The Best At Being Me

by Lisa Combs • illustrated by Pam Fraizer

*Dedicated to all of my former students
and many other special children I've known who inspired this book
with their unique and amazing interests and talents!*

No part of this publication may be reproduced
in whole or part, or stored in a retrieval system,
or transmitted in any form, or by any means,
electronic, mechanical, photocopying, recording, or otherwise,
without written permission of the author and illustrator.

ISBN-13: 978-1546314783

© 2017, Best Friend Books, LLC

Printed in the USA.

The Best At Being Me

by Lisa Combs • illustrated by Pam Fraizer

Some folks can spell almost any words,
and arrange them from A to Z.
I try my best
to pass my spelling tests,
but I'm the best at being me.

Some folks are good with numbers,
and they love their 1,2,3's.
I'm not good with amounts,
but I still count...
because I'm the best at being me!

Some folks can hit a baseball
as far as your eye can see.
I can't hit a home run,
but I can still have fun...
Because I'm the best at being me!

Some folks can sing 8 octaves
and a perfect middle C.
My attempt at a tune
sounds like a howl at the moon.
But I'm the best at being me!

Some folks are good at hang gliding
across the sky, over the sea.
I'll stick around
and cheer from the ground,
but I'm the best at being me.

Some folks can talk in front of crowds
without getting wobbly, nervous knees.
But when I try,
my mouth gets dry.
But I'm the best at being me.

Some folks can draw most anything
and paint the scenery.
When I painted Bob,
he came out a blob!
But I'm the best at being me.

I'm good at making people laugh,
and pretending to be a wizard...
and seeing pictures in the clouds,
and playing with my lizard!

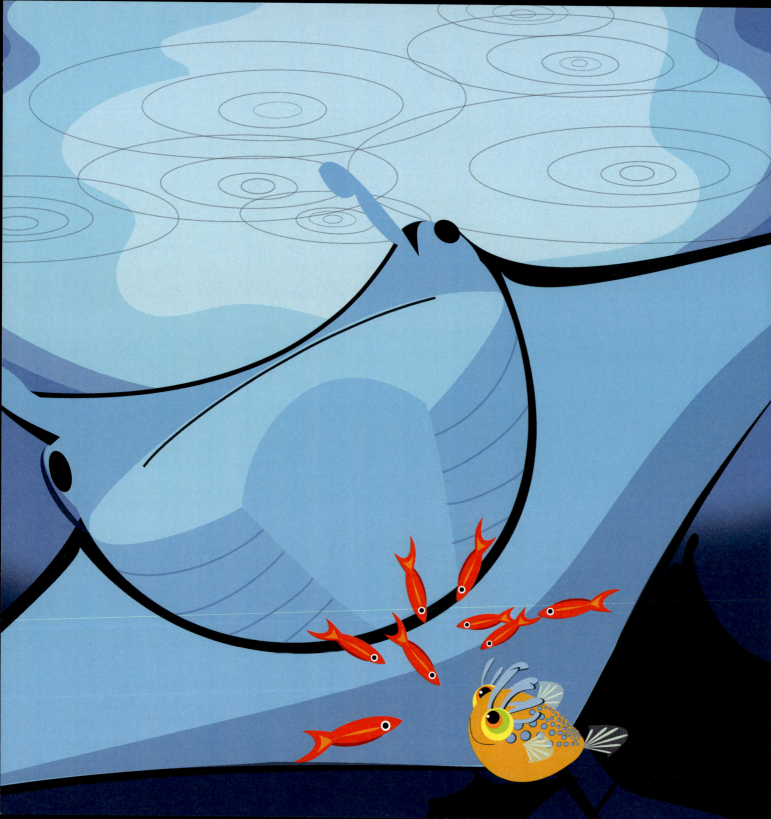

I'm good at running the vacuum,
and playing with my trains!
I'm good at building blanket forts,
and listening to the rain.

I'm good at doing experiments,
and making things from scratch!
I'm good at designing outfits
(although they might not always match).

So what else am I good at?
There's one thing more to see!
I'm an awesome friend,
by your side 'til the end.
And I'm the best at being me!

Lisa Combs

is an educator, advocate for children,
and owner of Combs Educational Consulting, Ltd.
To learn more about Lisa, visit her website at:
www.combseducationalconsulting.com

Pam Fraizer

is a graphic artist, illustrator,
and owner of FraizerDesigns, LLC.
To see more of Pam's art, visit her website at:
www.fraizerdesigns.org

Visit us both at www.bestfriendbooks.com